The Six Figure Sharpener

W. L. Laney

Copyright © 2014 WL Laney
All rights reserved.
ISBN:1502584379
ISBN-13:9781502584373

DEDICATION

To Coleen, my wife of 43 years, my two children – four grandchildren, four great-grandchildren and all the people who have purchased my Diamond Rose Superior Sharpening System.

Contents

DEDICATION..3
Introduction..7
Chapter 1 – Is a six-figure income realistic? 13
Chapter 2 – Choosing the proper equipment 21
Chapter 3 – Haircutting Scissors Sales..29
Chapter 4 – How to market your products and services..................37
Chapter 5 – Providing customer service. 45
Chapter 6 – Build your financial future 53
Chapter 7 – Passion – Passion comes before profit........................59

Introduction

My purpose in writing this book is twofold. First, it is designed as an educational tool. I will provide the information about the various aspects of the scissors sharpening industry you need to make an intelligent decision as to whether you want to be involved in this industry or not.

Second, it is a soft-sales pitch. My goal is to help you start a profitable scissors sharpening and sales business using our patented **Diamond Rose Superior Sharpening Machine** and top quality **Musashi Shears.** Please understand that my sales pitch is as honest as I can make it, but I admit I am prejudiced about the beauty industry.

With the **Diamond Rose Superior Sharpening System** you can earn an above average income focusing on this segment of the scissors sharpening industry. Based on my years of experience as a business broker, business consultant and mergers and acquisitions consultant, I believe the **Diamond Rose Superior Sharpening System** provides an unbeatable business opportunity in the following three areas.

It is a recession proof industry in a clean, healthy work environment. In addition to that, it has a nearly unlimited upside potential due to the vast number of beauty salons and barbershops all staffed with haircutting professionals who need scissors sharpened routinely and new scissors.

The cost of entry is significantly less than the typical franchise. (It is not a franchise, so there are no franchise or royalty fees now or in the future.) The time required to get started is extremely short. There is no college degree or special licensing requirements for the startup. The income potential is significantly better than 90% of the career opportunities available in the United States at this time.

First, let's start with my credentials.

I learned how to sharpen scissors in 1965. An elderly gentleman in Tucson, Arizona asked me to ride with him one day while I was visiting from the state of Washington. He wanted help spotting businesses that might need scissors sharpened.

So, as he drove, I watched for beauty salons, barbershops, upholstery shops, florists, tailors and alterations shops. As the day progressed, I became fascinated with both the amount of money he made and the ease of earning it which he demonstrated using his scissors sharpening machine.

When I spotted a potential prospect my white-haired gentleman friend would pull up his old pickup truck in front of the business, and we would both jump out to go in. The sales pitch he used was as simple as could be, he'd ask, "Do you have scissors you need sharpened?"

If they did, my friend sharpened the scissors in just a few minutes time, charged the owner $.50 a pair and we went back to his truck and repeated the process over and over throughout the day.

Before you laugh at the idea of making $.50 a pair, you need to understand that in 1965, gas sold for $.31 a gallon, a first-class postage stamp was five cents and you could purchase the typical new home for $21,000.

My friend taught me how to use his machine to sharpen scissors and then loaned it to me for my return trip to the state of Washington.

I had decided to move to Arizona and was making the trip back to Washington to pick up my belongings before returning to Arizona. Not long after the move I began traveling around the country as an evangelist for my church.

The scissors sharpening machine was a godsend. I was able to pay all of my travel expenses, and more, simply by sharpening scissors as I travelled from town to town. This enabled me to help many of the small churches that normally would not have been able to pay for my services.

The sharpening machine I used was a Foley-Belsaw grinder style sharpening machine, which worked perfectly, since at that time all the hair cutting scissors had beveled edges.

Now fast-forward my story to 2001. I was living in Chandler, Arizona. My Mergers and Acquisition Company had a suite of offices on the top floor of a major downtown office building. My wife, Coleen, and I had just finished building our dream home about 5 miles away in an exclusive gated community. I was a member of a local country club and golf course, which was about a half-mile away from the office. My son, William, worked with me in the office, my daughter and son-in-law owned a business about an hour and a half away, we attended a great church and "life was good".

As you are most likely well aware, just when we think we have it made, things can take an unexpected turn. I was working on what was going to be our "retire in ease" business deal when the terrorist attacks of September 11, 2001 turned the financial world upside down.

First my "retire in ease" business deal died on the vine. Then my entire business followed suit. Without an income, it was not long before our house went into foreclosure. Later in the book I will talk about the importance of "attitude", and the value of being willing to "do whatever it takes" and why you should never give up regardless of the circumstances.

For me, it was necessary to face reality. Since I had sunk everything I had into my "retire in ease" business transaction I was now broke. It takes time for the bank to actually throw you out of a house when they foreclose. But during the middle of the summer in Arizona keeping the electricity on and the air-conditioning running is pretty much a necessity, as is having the cash to buy groceries.

Although I had lots of experience selling real estate, operating a business brokerage and working as a mergers and acquisition consultant – all of those options have medium to long ramp-up times before money starts rolling in. In my condition at that moment, I did not have the luxury of time on my side.

They say "necessity is the mother of invention". When you combine necessity with desperation you'll get an idea of how I felt. I looked back over my nearly 40 years of business experience and I remembered the scissors sharpening business.

Really, in my mind at that time, I didn't think of it as a business but rather a short-term moneymaking activity that could generate cash immediately. There was just one small problem. I no longer had a scissors sharpening machine. That's where the idea of "do whatever it takes" came into play. I went to a job placement agency to find some kind of temporary work so I could meet my immediate needs for cash. The only thing I found was a job as "Mr. Peanut". Because of my desperate situation I took it.

Now, picture this, here I was Mr. successful business owner, country club member, church board member and gated community homeowner standing in front of a new Walmart dressed as Mr. Peanut passing out bags of peanuts for their grand opening. Oh, and by the way, I forgot to mention that I drove to work in my Mercedes convertible without air-conditioning. It had quit and I had no money to get it fixed.

The only good part of that story was the Mr. Peanut costume came with a mask that covered my face so no one coming into the Walmart knew it was me.

That was <u>step one</u> of my effort to buy groceries, pay utilities and buy a scissors sharpening machine. <u>Step two</u> was a garage sale. <u>Step three</u> was a trip to the local pawn shop – all because I knew I could solve my immediate cash needs if I could just get my hands on a scissors sharpening machine. I knew from experience that hairstylists, tailors, alterations shops, dog groomers and florists all had scissors that needed to be sharpened and they would give me cash today when I completed the sharpening.

For me, the answer was in the words of Ruth Stafford Peal, wife of the Rev. Norman Vincent Peal who said,

"Find a need, and fill it."

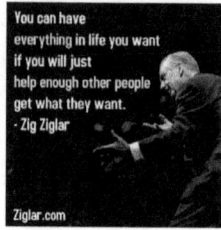

There is a point that many people miss, particularly when they are in a time of need. One of the best ways to solve your needs is to help other people solve their needs. I like the way Zig Ziglar said it,

"You can have everything life has to offer, if you will just help enough other people get what they want."

I've told you all of this to help you understand – regardless of your current financial needs, the business opportunity I am discussing, can be a solution for you as well. I moved from the depths of despair, foreclosure, bankruptcy and the loss of my business through a process of "doing whatever it took" – to having it all back and more in less than four years. I now have a larger home, a Mercedes convertible (with air conditioning that works) and a new very satisfying business. My new business is based on helping other people succeed in starting their own businesses.

Let me move on from here and describe how you can earn an above average income in beauty industry.

Chapter 1 – Is a six-figure income realistic?

"Optimism is what will drive you to keep going when things turn sour. Optimism will make you do great things because you believe things will improve. If you have optimism, you will always find the right direction".

Unknown

What do you need to be successful? As a matter of fact how do you define success in the first place? Is there an income level you need, a neighborhood you want to live in, or an occupation that will meet your definition of success?

What is your perception of the scissors sharpening industry? Do you immediately think of some scruffy looking individual driving around in a beat up old van? Or do you think of a well-dressed professional going from salon to salon providing a much-needed service?

One day my son, William, was making a deposit at his bank. A new "manager in training" – teller waited on him. The teller, just trying to be friendly, asked William what he did for a living. William responded, "I sharpen haircutting scissors." The "manager in training" rolled his eyes and his body language said, *"I'm sorry I bothered trying to be friendly, I only want to develop relationships with successful people."*

The reason I know this story is because of what happened next. William said, "This deposit is what I earned today." Now, based on the size of the deposit, the "manager in training's" body language changed to one of surprise and embarrassment for his previous attitude. Hopefully this "manager in training" learned not to judge a book by its cover.

As I said earlier, attitude is one of the keys to success in life. It is not the only one, but it's definitely one of the most important keys to finding business success.

A former employee, Jan, is probably one of the best examples of how your attitude is going to impact your success.

If you feel less than professional about yourself it will be reflected in your body language and in your conversations with stylists. They will sense that you do not believe their needs are important. You will find it very difficult to build a loyal customer base if they do not believe you are sincerely interested in helping them solve their problems.

A few years ago I hired Jan to sell shears in our area and to set sharpening appointments for a local sharpener. I was excited about Jan's potential because she had previously worked in the industry calling on beauty spa owners. The success that she had in her previous job was nothing short of phenomenal.

Much to my dismay, Jan was a total failure during the short period of time that she worked for me. Her lack of sales had me totally baffled until I had a heart to heart conversation with her. According to Jan, she couldn't relate (have respect for) to our customers, the individual stylists. In her prior position she worked only with the owners. As we talked it became clear to me that Jan did not respect the individual stylist, our customer, and as a result they did not respect Jan and were unwilling to buy from her.

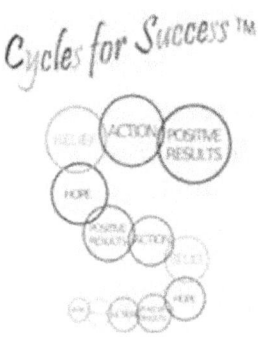

The good news is, you can develop a positive attitude about yourself, your occupation/vocation, your products, services and most importantly your customers.

In my book **"The Self-Administered Attitude Transplant"** I discuss what

I call the "**Cycles for Success.**" The basis of the book is actually a prescription I developed for a very talented individual who failed as a scissors sharpener.

The first step is "**Hope**" – I hope for success. Another way to describe it is desire. Start with a desire. What is it that you really want the most? And then build on that. The stronger the desire, the more stable your base for building a successful business will be.

The next step is "**Belief.**" It is vital to believe in yourself. If you do not believe you can swim across the lake, you will not dive in. The last thing anyone wants is to swim halfway across the lake only to discover they can't make it the rest of the way. Who wants to drown in the middle of the lake? This is true in all parts of our life. If you do not believe – if you don't have faith, you will not make the attempt.

Perhaps you need someone in your life who will "burn your boats." When the ancient Greeks reached the enemy's shoreline, the first order of the commander was, to burn the boats. It was a very effective way to motivate the troops. They were committed. There was no turning back. The only possibility was in victory over the enemy.

If someone burns your boat for you, or if you have a deep enough belief in your project that you will burn your own boat, you will have a much better chance of success.

The next step is "**Action**" – there is a Bible passage that says, *"Faith without works is dead"*. How true it is, you can believe all you want but until you take action nothing is going to happen. Start with a small "action step". It is important that you build self-confidence. If you

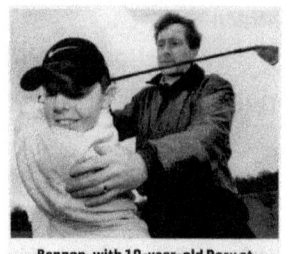

Bannon, with 10-year-old Rory at Holywood Golf Club outside Belfast.

try to take too large a step it can have an adverse effect on your life. When you are starting on a journey toward success you need positive reinforcement.

One of the best examples I have heard recently is about Rory McIlroy. At the time of this writing Rory is the number one ranked golfer in the world. When he was age 7 Rory's father, Gerry, and golf instructor, Michael Bannon, devised a plan to instill confidence in young Rory.

They developed a special scorecard for him. The first hole was listed as a par eight. The second hole was a par six. The third was a par seven. And so on throughout the balance of the course. On that basis, Rory was shooting 4-under for nine holes before he was 10.

Successfully taken "**Action steps**" lead to number four in our cycles for success –"**Positive Results**". And now you can see why I call it the cycles for success. "**Positive Results**" lead to more "**Hope**" and the cycle repeats.

As important as "**Attitude**" is for business success, it is a lot like "**Hope**" in our Cycles for Success. There are a number of other very important items that must be added to your positive attitude, before you become a "**Six Figure Sharpener.**"

You will also need:

- The proper equipment

- Appropriate training

- Support

- Confidence

- Competence

In the next chapter I will discuss the need for a very specific kind of equipment based on the way the scissors are manufactured.

Chapter 2 – Choosing the proper equipment

Accept yourself, your strengths, your weaknesses, your truths, and know what tools you have to fulfill your purpose."– Steve Maraboli, Life, the Truth, and Being Free

Before you select your sharpening machine you need to:

1. Make your selection of the industry segment you plan to serve.

2. Understand how the scissors used in that industry segment are manufactured.

3. Select the machine that will match those factory specifications.

In one of my other books, ***The Art of Professional Scissors Sharpening,*** I discuss the various industry segments and the type of sharpening machine that is required for each segment. If you would like an autographed copy please give our office a call 303-217-8660 extension 3. Or simply go to Amazon.com to order your personal copy.

For now I am going to make the assumption that you have decided on sharpening haircutting scissors for the beauty salons and barbershops in your area.

Most of the stylists and more and more barbers are using the better quality Japanese-style shears. It is important to understand that all shears are not equal. Although you could cut hair using a $5 pair of office scissors the results would be problematic.

In the beauty industry today, the most popular shear design is the Japanese Style Shear. Well over 85% of the shears you will see in barbershops and salons across the country will be Japanese Style shears. Our **Diamond Rose Superior Sharpening System** is designed specifically for the Japanese-style shear. However, it can also accommodate the German style shear, which makes up the balance of the shears in use.

What makes the Japanese-style shears so popular are three very important design components.

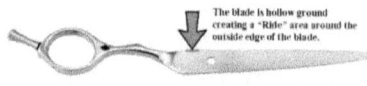

First: the inside of the blade is **hollow ground**. This means the center of the inside of the blade is ground down so it is lower than the edges. This creates what is called a "ride area" around the perimeter of the blade. This "ride area" must be perfectly flat and highly polished if you expect the scissors to cut and cut well.

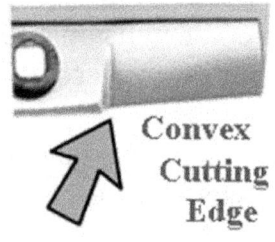

Second: The **convex edge**. The convex edge in conjunction with the ride area is designed to give the shears a cleaner, sharper cut. It also allows the stylist do what they call slide cutting. If you sharpen using a grinder style machine, you will destroy the convex edge replacing it with a bevel edge and then the stylist will not be able to slide cut. Actually, sharpening shears on a grinder converts the Japanese-style convex edge into an old German style bevel edge. The older German style bevel edge shear can typically be purchased for $50-$75. Whereas the Japanese-style shears will typically cost the stylist between $125.00 to $1,000 dollars or more.

Third: the **800 mm radius**. The Japanese-style shear has a slight curve in the blade from the hilt to the tip based on an 800 mm radius. If you were to draw a line following the curve in the blade you'd wind up with a circle about 6 feet in diameter. This curve adjusts the angle of attack and "holds the hair" in place while the scissors blades cut it. The old German style scissors have a straight blade and often have added a serrated edge on one blade designed to hold the hair in place while the other blade cuts through it. Although it was effective at holding the hair in place, it gave the scissors a "rough" cutting action and does not accommodate the "slide cutting" done by the majority of stylists. Slide cutting enables the stylist to give the hair a textured or feathered look instead of the "blunt" look accomplished with the old German style scissors.

Once you understand these design features of the most popular shears, I believe you're faced with an integrity issue – what machine will you purchase? If a sharpener knowingly sharpens a Japanese-style shear on a grinder style machine, they are altering the shape and design of the shear and therefore demonstrate a total lack of integrity.

Figure 1 Foley-Belsaw

Let's take a moment and go back to my personal story. Earlier, I told you I did what it took to buy a scissors-sharpening machine. It was a different brand than I had used

40 years earlier, but it was exactly the same design and worked exactly the same way.

I learned very soon that the design of the scissors had changed in my absence from the industry, but the design of the sharpening equipment had not changed to meet the design criteria of the more popular Japanese Style shear. You have heard that "necessity is the mother of invention." As soon as I started sharpening, with what I very quickly learned was antiquated equipment, I began a search for a sharpening machine that would allow me to sharpen the scissors without damaging the blade.

What I discovered was there was none. Besides the grinder that I had purchased, the only other alternative was a "flat hone" machine. The "flat hone" was able to maintain the convex edge on the Japanese Style shear but it did not accommodate the 800 mm radius, which I will talk about in just a moment.

Discovering that there was no other machine available I immediately went to work on trying to solve that issue. And from my desire to address that issue for the stylists the **Diamond Rose Superior Sharpening** machine was born.

By this time, I had been able to solve my short-term financial problems. I then turned my attention to the long-term. I've owned and operated a number of different businesses, one of which was a business brokerage; another was a merger and acquisition firm both of which gave me a very strong background in business and business startups.

I began working on developing the **Diamond Rose Superior Sharpening System.** The first step was to solve the machine issue. I hired an engineering firm, taught them how to sharpen scissors and then described exactly what I needed the machine to do. I laugh about this a lot when I tell people how easy the machine is to operate. I told the engineering firm to make it "idiot proof" so I could use it.

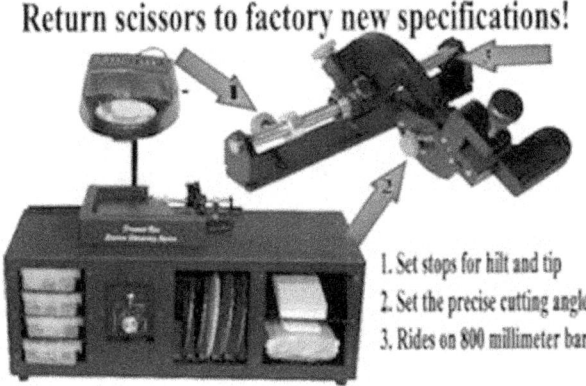

In truth, it is very easy to operate. The design of our clamp guide assembly takes all the guesswork out. It allows the operator to set stops for the tip and hilt of the blade, the cutting angle, and also provides the ability to center the 800 mm radius thereby maintaining or even restoring it. For a graphical illustration of how the machine works please go to YouTube and watch the video "**How to Sharpen Hair Scissors**".

http://www.youtube.com/user/BestBusinessOpp

This process and the resulting patented "**Diamond Rose Superior Sharpening Machine**" solved the machine issue. The next step was to acquire or develop a product to sell. The most logical product for a scissors sharpener to present to a hairstylist is haircutting scissors. If you are going to become a "**Six-Figure Sharpener**" you need to work long hours sharpening, or supplement your service income with product sales.

Chapter 3 – Haircutting Scissors Sales

"Everyone lives by selling something".

– Robert Louis Stevenson

For years, people have been saying you should work smarter not harder. The challenge with that is no one seems to have the formula for what is smarter.

From my perspective one of the nice things about getting older is the opportunity to have learned from both good and bad experiences. I have learned that commission sales efforts are one of the most highly rewarded activities on the planet.

It is amazing to me how many people call my office and say, "I just want to sharpen, I do not want to sell", or "I am not a salesman." The missing ingredient here is that they fail to realize if you can sell your services to the stylist, you can sell shears as well. Looking at it objectively, it's actually easier to sell shears than it is to sell the service.

When you talk to stylists about shears, they can see it, feel it, examine and try it. When you talk about your service, they have to trust you and take your word for the fact you will do a good job. You have to convince them that you are not going to ruin their expensive scissors as you sharpen them. Most stylists have had plenty of experience with scissors being ruined, so your story has to be very convincing.

I think the real issue is not that we don't want to be a salesman. I think, rather, it is we don't want to be viewed as the "typical sleazy salesman". As you consider setting up your new business, please consider yourself as a consultant to the professional hairstylist in terms of both sharpening and scissors for their use.

The premise of being a "**Six-Figure Sharpener**" revolves around setting up your personal home-based sales and service business. Any working hairstylist has scissors that need to be sharpened. That becomes your door opener to show and sell shears. One of the easiest ways to sell a pair of shears is to have the stylist use one of your demo shears while you are sharpening their dull scissors.

So let's talk about the **Musashi Shears** brand. **Musashi** is a proprietary brand, which we developed for the express purpose of providing purchasers of the **Diamond Rose Superior Sharpening System** a product to sell.

Let me give you two examples of how it can work for you. During the middle of the recent recession I made an exploratory trip to Cheyenne, Wyoming for a day. I wanted to be away from anybody in the Denver area who might know me or our sharpening systems and/or shears.

The day began with the drive from Castle Rock, Colorado to Cheyenne, Wyoming. Arriving at 10:00 AM, I used my cell phone navigation app to locate the nearest hair salon. Driving from salon to salon I spent 6-½ hours showing our Musashi Shears and sharpening for those who asked for scissors to be sharpened. I really did not want to spend the time sharpening, but because of the demand I ended up sharpening 10 pair of scissors at $35 each, plus I picked up a five-dollar tip. You will likely get more tips than I did, everyone seems to. I guess the stylists think I'm the owner of the parent company they don't need to tip me.

I went into each salon focused on showing and selling shears. As a result, I sold five pair of scissors for approximately $3,000. Two of the stylists who purchased shears took advantage of the 15% discount I offered for cash. The other three preferred our 18-month interest free payment option.Over the years our interest free payment option has been a huge hit with stylists. On the **Musashi Shears** easy pay plan the stylist can buy a $550.00 pair of scissors for approximately $30.00 per month. This option makes our top-quality shears affordable to any stylist who is working. Taking a dollar or two out of their tips every day enables them to save for and make their monthly installment with ease.

Please understand I am not promoting this level of income as a daily standard. It was a unique day and you should not expect to do it every day, however; it does show the possibilities. A more typical day is reflected in my visit to a salon here in the Denver area last week.

I entered the salon and opened my 30-shear display case to show the first stylist. I briefly said that we had some great shears and I had a sale, which would save money for purchases made today. The stylist said she was sorry but not interested in purchasing shears today. As I started to walk away toward the next stylist, she called me back and asked if I could sharpen her scissors.

I went to the car got my scissors sharpening system and return to the salon. I asked the stylist to try a pair of my demos while I sharpened her scissors. As I explained our interest free payment option she said yes, she would like to buy the pair that she was trying out.

Well, that set the stage and in about an hour and a half to an hour and 45 minutes I sharpened three more pair of scissors for a total of four pair earning $140.00 in sharpening fees. And, I sold another pair of scissors to one of the other girls I sharpened for. Both of the stylists on that particular day elected for our interest free payment option. We currently pay a 50% commission on scissors sold. Your income for that stop would have been approximately $500 in commissions and $140 in sharpening.

I think you can see why I recommend selling shears along with providing sharpening services for the individual stylists in the salons in your neighborhood. Without the commissions for the scissors sales, the income would have been $140.00 instead of $640.00.

As I alluded to earlier, our **Musashi Shears** are top quality Japanese-style haircutting scissors. I routinely have the shears tested at a Denver metallurgical lab to assure the manufacturer is staying true to our stringent specifications for the manufacture of the shears. We have approximately 120 different models and lengths for stylists to choose from.

That means we have more different styles in both right and left handed shears than most of the competitors I am aware of. The fact that we allow the stylist to try the scissors in the salon is a huge benefit to them. Stylist appreciate being able to "test-drive" scissors prior to buying them.

Stylists typically have four choices when it comes to purchasing their most important tool.

1. They can go to the local beauty supply and by a pair there. The problem with this option is twofold, first, the typical beauty supply house does not have the better quality shears available and second, the stylists are not allowed to try the scissors before they buy them.

2. They can buy scissors when they attend a beauty show. The challenge here is again, they cannot try the shears out. The second issue is they have no place to go after the show if they have a problem with the shear.

3. They can wait for a scissors sharpener to come to their salon which shears to sell. Typically the scissors being offered by itinerant sharpeners are a lower quality shear and are often times over priced at that.

4. They can purchase the scissors online. Here again, they cannot try the scissors out before purchasing.

This is why we have such great luck selling the **Musashi Shears**. One, they are a great quality shear with a lifetime warranty against any factory defect. Two, they are able to try the shears before purchasing. And three, we can offer them a cash discount or our easy, interest free payment plan.

Chapter 4 – How to market your productsand services

"Beauty salons have proven to be a recession-proof industry in the United States. Although sales had declined from 2008 highs, they remain robust with long term positive forecast. The market is distributed widely across America, with a concentration in the Northeast and Midwest. The US Labor Department estimates employment will increase the industry, in the United States will increase 20% between 2008–2014, with greatest employment growth from skin care specialists".

Wikipedia

There are approximately 400,000 beauty salons in the United States. We calculate that rural area salons have between two and three stylists working. In the larger towns and cities that number goes up to approximately 5 stylists or more per salon. This calculation suggests your potential market to be about 1.5 million people using haircutting scissors.

Of course you are not going to work the entire country. Our research and experience shows that if you follow our system and build a loyal customer base close to where you live, you only need about 300 salons.

Before we discuss how to market to your target area there are a couple of issues that need to be addressed. A common misconception in the sharpening world is that stylists are not loyal. It doesn't take very many conversations with professional hairstylists to ascertain why this misconception persists in the industry today.

Walk into any salon and ask a stylist about their experience with scissors sharpeners. Some will say, "We don't have anybody coming in anymore." Or "We used to have a guy coming around but he retired last year." Or "I don't trust anybody to sharpen my scissors, I just buy a new pair." Or "I send mine to the factory." Or "If I let someone else sharpen my scissors it will void my warranty." Occasionally someone will say, "I have a great sharpener who takes care of my scissors".

I don't want to bore you with all the horror stories I have heard in the field. But there are a couple I would like to relate to you so that you can get a feel for the enormous need there is for professional scissors sharpening.

One day in Phoenix I had been called to a Salon Suites facility by a stylist who wanted her scissors sharpened. When I arrived I discovered another sharpener was already there sharpening as well. I sharpened the shears for the stylist who had called and was calling on the other individual suites when I walked into Nancy's suite. She looked at me with eyes that spoke both discovery and distress. "Oh! That's what happened!"

Then Nancy related her story. She had given her scissors to the other sharpener's wife thinking she was sending them to me because she had seen me come into the building. Nancy had just spent $30.00 on the other sharpener and now her scissors would not cut. I gave her a discount because I felt so bad about the situation. But when I left her suite, Nancy's scissors cut perfectly.

This story will help you understand what I am about to explain. The reason stylists are not loyal is because sharpeners using antiquated equipment are damaging and or ruining their scissors. The stylists are paying to have their scissors sharpened and then discovering after the sharpener leaves their salon that the scissors won't cut.

One of the worst cases I have heard about happened to Sandra in Scottsdale, AZ. Sandra gave her scissors to a sharpener who finished sharpening her scissors; put them on the counter for her, collected his money and left the salon. A little while later when she picked up her scissors, Sandra discovered the sharpener had actually broken one of the blades completely in two.

One of her coworkers reminded her that she had paid by check. Sandra immediately called her bank only to find the sharpener had already been there and cashed the check. And of course, he did not leave a business card with a contact phone number.

A year or so ago, I received a call from Sam, a sharpener from Chicago who was interested in the **Diamond Rose Superior Sharpening System**. Sam did not follow through with the purchase because he thought we were too expensive.

Let me tell you about Sam. Sam explained to me he had been a "successful" sharpener for 20 years. I was just about to compliment him, when he went on to say he covered a four state area.

Remember I told you, working a 300-salon market area is the ideal. Because of the number of stylists and the fact they need their scissors sharpened every 90 days. That is as large a group of stylists as you can competently service on a consistent basis. The four state area Sam was covering included more than 35,000 salons.

The reason Sam had to travel that far was really quite simple. He needed enough time for the stylists to forget he was the guy that damaged their scissors the last time he was in the salon.

Now, about our system being too expensive. If Sam could have understood the investment in equipment and training would have saved huge amounts of time and particularly travel expenses. Sam could have spent many more nights at home instead of in hotels traveling his four state area. Had he used the right equipment, he could have built a loyal customer base in the 300 salons closest to his home;

he would also have built a business that could have been sold for a nice retirement fund. To say nothing about the benefit he would have brought to his stylist customers.

Going "cheap" is rarely the best course of action. Quality counts in both products and services. I would advise you here and now to make a commitment to providing the very best quality services and products to your customers. You will do a better job for your customers and in so doing you will build a much more valuable business.

How to build a territory

Building a successful "territory" of loyal stylists is the best way to assure yourself of repeat business and long-term success. Start by selecting the 300 salons closest to where you live. This can be accomplished using the Yellow Pages or other type of directory such as Yelp that will identify name, address, phone number and possibly the manager/owner's name.

Your territory boundaries do not necessarily need to be precise. The main concern in setting the boundaries is so that you do not overreach your capability of providing the best quality of service to your chosen territory for the long term.

We are routinely asked by prospective purchasers, "Where can I utilize your system?" The answer is, almost anywhere. Your best results will be in focusing on the 300 salons closest to your home. The major problem with working outside of your chosen 300-salon target area is follow up.

Let's say you take a summer trip or vacation and sharpen scissors all along the way. You will have created what I call sharpening orphans. These are people that have learned about the quality of the **Diamond Rose Shears Superior Sharpening System**. And quite frankly, they want you back when their scissors get dull.

I believe the best solution is to focus on your target audience, earn your money, then let your vacation be a non-working vacation. Leave the machine at home and go enjoy yourself.

Now that we described your 300-salon territory let's talk about service. You may be able to call on each salon in your chosen area the first time around in 30 days. Don't worry about the fact that you will normally do a 90-day routine. Go back to the first salon and start over. This time it may take you 60 days because you will be sharpening more shears. Repeat the process the third time around and it may take 90 days. The more the stylists experience your quality sharpening, the more they will want you to do the work and will in fact, become loyal customers.

I think it's a great idea to use some proven marketing tactics. For example you may print 10 squares on the back of your card and explain to the stylist that the 10th sharpening will be free. Or, you may find out the stylist's birthdate and offer a discounted sharpening for a birthday present. The most important thing next to the quality of your service is to develop a relationship with the individual stylist.

Getting calls to come to the salon by a loyal customer almost always means developing new business because the other stylists who have not used you yet, will take advantage of your services while you are visiting the salon. Past customers are an even greater help when it comes to selling shears. I love it when I am talking to a stylist in a salon with other stylists who have purchased our **Musashi Shears** in the past. They are great salespeople for me.

A 300 salon territory will have between 900 and 1,500 stylists all of whom need their scissors sharpened on an average of four times per year. In addition to that they also need their texturizing shears sharpened once or twice a year. That is six sharpening's per stylist every year. If you use 1,200 as a number of stylists and $35 for each sharpening you are looking at $252,000 of potential sharpening income for the year.

No, you are not going to get everybody. But I think if you examine your market and set a realistic goal and then do everything in your power to serve the stylists in your 300-salon area you will be able to see great success as a "**Six-Figure Sharpener**".

In addition to your sharpening income there is also the commissions you can earn on the scissors sales. Let's use the same 1,200 stylists, who the manufacturers say, buy an average of one new shear per year. Again, it is doubtful that you will be able to control the entire market. If you did sell 1,200 pair of shears with a 50% commission against our average sales price of $550.00 – there is a potential of $330,000 per year in scissors sales commissions.

Set your goals, show your shears, and provide excellent customer service. These steps will enable you to build a very successful home-based business in this unique segment of the multi-billion-dollar beauty industry.

Chapter 5 –
Providing customer service.

"There is only one boss. The customer. And he can fire everybody in the company from the chairman on down, simply by spending his money somewhere else".

Sam Walton

We live in a day where it seems "customer service" is more of an oxymoron than a reality. The good news about that is, it takes very little effort to stand out in the crowd. In my lifetime of business activity I have discovered that customer service can often make up for other weaknesses in my business applications. People like and appreciate the fact that I am there to help them even if everything else seems to be going wrong.

I would like to share a number of customer service ideas and practices that I have found very successful. These are not given in any particular order other than this is the order that they came to mind.

Number one– prompt response. There is nothing more frustrating to your customer than having a need, calling you, and then waiting for you to finally show up. The waiting period is where all the bad stuff happens. Your customer begins to think that you're not going to come, or you're not going to take care of the issue, or worse, they spent their money and it is wasted. When I get a call my typical response is: "tell me what's wrong" – when they respond with their issue, the first thing I say is "That will never do – let's get a time scheduled so I can come out and get _____ taken care of".

Now we have a time scheduled, we have the customer relieved, and the problem is not "festering" into an issue where I simply cannot make the customer happy. An additional benefit to this practice is that it has a huge value in helping to build a long-term relationship with that particular salon. The rest of the stylists get a first-hand look at the quality of your service, and the fact that you are there to take care of whatever issues come up. One thing that many people don't seem to realize is that your customer is not insisting on perfection, they just want to be taken care of. They understand that "life happens". What they really appreciate is you being there to help them through whatever it is that has happened.

Number two– genuine concern. Genuine concern is a customer service response that cannot be "faked". Ask yourself this question. "Which is more important, a happy customer or money in my pocket?" Here is the good part; a happy customer will mean money in your pocket. Perhaps not today but over the long haul, happy customers mean more profit for you.

Some people wear attitude on their sleeve. Your customer will see through that kind of an attitude. They will also recognize an "owner's attitude" when all of your dealings with them demonstrate you are genuinely concerned about meeting their needs. There is probably no better way to create loyalty than by meeting the needs of your customer.

Number three– money-back policy. Great customer service always has a money-back policy. I think we all understand the importance of having a money-back guarantee on our products and services. But, do you understand, if it is not a money-back guarantee with a genuine smile, you may as well keep your money. I'm sure you have experienced the same as I have – they made you fight so hard to get your money back, you are so angry that even though you got your money back you vowed never to shop there again.

Number four– quality work. There is no substitute for quality workmanship. The **Diamond Rose Superior Sharpening System** allows you to do precision sharpening at a quality level unmatched by any competitor. It is still imperative that you pay attention to detail. Sloppy work will only yield sloppy results.

I recall many years ago in my high school shop class the instructor repeatedly warned us to do a thorough job of sanding prior to putting the finish on the wood. He said the finish would not cover up a lack of sanding, but rather would highlight the sloppy job.

You will find it is the same when sharpening haircutting scissors. If you see some small issue when you test the scissors, take time fix-it. Make it right. If you don't, the stylist will spot the problem immediately, and you can potentially lose a loyal customer simply because you did not pay attention to detail.

Number five– don't blame your customer. Even if it is the customer's fault, don't point your finger at them. This is a great time for education. If you educate without lecturing or blaming them, they will see it was their fault and appreciate the fact that you did not try to blame them. You have broad shoulders; let them be seen by assuming the fault even though it was not yours. I know this seems like a little thing but it has a huge impact in the workplace.

Number six – the customer is always right. There is an old adage that says "the customer is always right". Throughout my career I have added to that,

"If your customer is not right, they will soon be someone else's customer who lets them be right."

Of course, we all know the customer is not always right, but if we do not treat them as if they are right, they will go to our competitor. It really is that simple. Successful business owners understand and operate on that principle. Will people take advantage of you? Without a doubt, a few may take advantage of you. I can tell you from my experience the individuals taking advantage of you will be a small minority. Your principle of making the customer always right will reap huge dividends as you build your business.

Number seven-educate – Educate – educate – educate. Education, "sharing your knowledge", can be one of the greatest tools in building customer loyalty. You want to be the "go-to" person in your targeted marketing area. Selling your product and service is easiest when you spend time educating your customers. Providing information, explaining why it is important and talking about how you can solve their problem can flow seamlessly when you are educating your prospect and/or customer. Remembering the days that I owned a real estate brokerage everything was location – location – location. If you want to be a **"Six-Figure Sharpener"**, it all has to be education – education – education.

Number seven– don't badmouth the competition. Quality work, excellent customer service and a positive "customer focused" attitude are far better than trying to run down the competition. There are some things you should bear in mind before you say anything negative about the competition. You may be speaking to a relative of the competition. It's possible you are talking to the competition's best friend. Without doubt whatever you say will get back to your competition and you could be starting a war that no one can win.

As described earlier, "education" is your best tool. The more you describe the quality of what you do the easier it will be for your customer or prospective customer to see the competition just can't stand up to the precision sharpening you will provide.

In one major metro area a regional manager for one of the franchise salons told her store managers to tell any sharpener coming in that, "My uncle does all the sharpening for our shop." The reality was the regional manager had a good friend who was a scissors sharpener and was doing their best to move all of the business from the stylists to her friend. Personally, I thought it was pretty funny although creative on the part of the regional manager. Stick with the education, quality work and a positive attitude you will be able to overcome any competition.

The only real competition you will ever have is someone else with the **Diamond Rose Superior Sharpening Machine**. U.S. patent #7,118,466,B2 provides complete protection for our ability to match factory specifications.

Excluding our sharpening system there are two basic types of machines available, one is a **"grinder"** and the other is a **"flat hone".** Using a grinder destroys the convex edge on the Japanese-style shear replacing it with a bevel edge. To put that into perspective – if a stylist spends $200 to $800 dollars on a Japanese-style shear – sharpening on a grinder will make it cut exactly the same as a $50-$75 low end barber scissors.

There can be no argument here. A bevel edge blade will not cut like a convex edge blade. The stylist paid extra money to get a convex edge blade. Sharpening on a grinder ruins it completely.

The flat hone machine may match the convex edge but the process of sharpening on a flat hone, straightens the 800 mm radius. When that happens, the scissors will "push" the hair when the stylist tries to cut through it. This adds to the stylist's fatigue at the end of the day because it took longer to do each haircut. It also cost the stylist money because they were able to do fewer cuts.

Number eight – personal hygiene. I am embarrassed to even include this section. The problem is too many people don't think about personal hygiene when working with the public. It is not just scissors sharpeners, but hairstylist and their customers as well.

It is very difficult to talk with somebody who is blowing onion, garlic breath or even cigarette smokein your face, for that matter. And please don't get close to me with your bad body odor.

As a scissors sharpener it is particularly important to keep your hands and fingernails clean. They do get dirty during the sharpening process. Which means you should wash your hands prior to returning the scissors to the stylist. It is not very professional to be pointing out the quality of your sharpening with fingers and nails coated in buffing compound or residue from your abrasive disk as a result of the sharpening process.

Number nine – professional language. Do not risk offending your customer or prospective customer with your language. You may hear stylists in the back room using language that would embarrass the proverbial sailor. That does not mean you should use the same language. You should also restrict your conversation to business or business related topics. Two areas to specifically avoid are politics and religion.

Chapter 6 –
Build your financial future

"It is an awesome thing to comprehend the magnitude of the fact that what a human being dreams and imagines can be realized. The power of that truth needs to be directed toward our creation of a future that is worthy of true human value and the world civilization".

Vanna Bonta

Owning your own business can yield tremendous benefits. The following 10 benefits are some of the more popular but certainly not all of the benefits you will receive by starting your own scissors sharpening and sales business.

1. **Get Paid What You Are Worth.** One of the problems with working for someone else is the pay scale. Most jobs do not pay what you are worth to the employer rather they pay the minimum possible. Actually, most jobs pay what your replacement is willing to work for. That is why the unions fought NAFTA so hard. They were afraid of the low pay scales in Mexico. When you own your own business, you set the pay scale. You provide your services and you are rewarded according to your contribution to the project you are working on. There is no employer taking his cut on your income.

2. **Set Your Own Hours**. When you are the boss, you can set your own hours. Of course there is always the limitation of your customer's requirements, such as when the shop is open. But other than that, the clock is yours. Are you an early starter? Start your day when you want to get up and get going. Are you a night owl? That is OK too. There is no one telling you to punch a clock. You are your own boss. The flip side can have some serious consequences. If you are not a self-starter, who is going to "boss" you? If you cannot discipline yourself, you should not own your own business. There is no one telling you what and when or how. You have to "boss" yourself.

3. **Choose Your Vacation Time**. This is a huge advantage. There is no one else pulling seniority for the days off you want. That special event across the country or around the world will not escape you because you could

not get the time off. You are the boss! Take the vacation when you want and for as long as you want. There is no waiting until you have been on the job five years before you get three weeks of vacation. You are the boss; take six weeks if you like the time is yours.

4. **Take Time Off For Family**. If you are tired of missing your children's school functions, consider this important benefit of being your own boss. When you own the company, you can take the time off when you need it. Whether it's your niece getting married, your son playing in his little league finals, your friend is in the hospital... the list goes on and on, it is your company, it is your time, use it the way you want.

5. **Do What You Enjoy Doing**. This benefit of business ownership is absolutely unlimited. You can do what you enjoy and make more money doing it. Do you like helping people? Consider a business like a scissors sharpening and sales business. You can help professional hair stylists with one of their basic needs... shears. You can restore them to factory new cutting condition. You can sell our fine Musashi Shears at an affordable factory direct price. Or, if you like fly-fishing, you can start a guide service and take other people fly-fishing with you and they will pay all the expenses and pay you as well. Do what you enjoy. See the possibilities? Our business opportunity gives you a success track to run on and can provide an above average income. With the money you earn and the time you can take off, go fly-fishing on your own without having to take a bunch of complete strangers fishing with you!

6. **Get Away From Office Politics**. Fire your boss, or co-worker or whoever is bugging you on your current

job. When you own your own business, you control the office politics. You set the stage for how the company will be run, how you will treat customers and how you will treat your employees if you have any. Take control of your working environment and enjoy your work. You can have so much fun running your own business it won't seem like work. And.... you will make more money.

7. **Enjoy Business Tax Advantages**. Owning your own business comes with a whole passel of tax advantages. They range from write-offs to tax credits for a variety of expenses like equipment purchases and providing employment to the handicapped. Talk to your tax consultant to be sure you take full advantage of the tax benefits of business ownership. A scissors sharpening and sales business is largely a cash business which some may take advantage of as well. Before deciding not to report all your income however, please read the caveat about when it is time to sell in the next section.

8. **Build Business Equity**. One of the most exciting aspects of owning your own business is the equity you can build. Working for someone else allows you to build a retirement fund depending on whom you work for. Some companies have "great" retirement plans once you become vested. That is, if the company does not go bankrupt or fire you before you are fully vested. These are at best long term advantages. When you own your own business, you are building equity with each stage of your growth. Generally if a business has been operated successfully for three or more years it is worth from three to five times its net income. Earn $100,000 each year and the business can be worth $300,000 to $500,000 when you decide to sell. There

are not many company retirement programs worth $300,000 to $500,000 after you have worked for as little as three years. Here is the caveat about reporting all your income. If you don't report it, you can't prove it to a prospective buyer. Personally, I don't want to save a few tax dollars on unreported income and lose triple what I saved or more when I sell the business. (Of course there is never a guarantee of what kind of multiple you might get when you decide it is the right time to sell your business.)

9. **Get The Respect You Deserve**. As a business owner, you get a level of respect not generally given to the "worker." There is a "feel good" aura about who you are and what you do. While it does not have a dollar amount attached to it, it fits right in with the good feeling you get helping others meet their goals.

10. **Enjoy Personal and Business Satisfaction**. There is no plaque or company award that matches the feeling you get running your own successful business. Helping people, enjoying freedom to do the things in life that really matter, having the means to provide for your family, building an equity base which guarantees your independence in retirement all bring a sense of satisfaction you will never enjoy working for the other guy. Take control of your own destiny. Build your own business.

If you like, Diamond Rose Shears, LLC can help. We have a proven success track to run on. For more detail, go to www.diamondroseshears.biz. Or simply call our office at 303-217-8660 Ext. 3.

Chapter 7 – Passion – Passion comes before profit.

"Passion is one great force that unleashes creativity, because if you're passionate about something, then you're more willing to take risks".

Yo-Yo Ma

Passion is the strong emotion applied to a person, a pursuit or a thing. Passion is an intense emotion, a compelling feeling, an enthusiasm, or desire for something. The term is also often applied to a lively or eager interest in or admiration for a proposal, cause, or activity or even love.

Passion can be expressed as a feeling of unusual excitement, enthusiasm or compelling emotion towards a subject, idea, person, or object. A person is said to have a passion for something when he has a strong positive affinity for it. A love for something and a passion for something are often used synonymously.

I have sold every customer I talked to about a promotional program our company is offering to new customers. Some of my sales staff, on the other hand, struggled to "give away" the product we offered in this promotion. What is the difference?

Passion... I am passionate about our products and services. I understand that our service saves the customer's most important tool for doing their job. I know our product is superior to the competition and is priced lower than any competitor of similar quality. This knowledge empowers me when talking about our products and services. It also comes through on a subliminal basis to the customer. They believe because I believe.

What do you believe about your product or service? Can you be passionate about it from both a quality and price standpoint? If not, you really need to find another job or find a way to develop a passion.

Here are three steps to help you develop your passion for your business.

Step 1: Learn about your customer. What are the needs your product or service will meet? What is most important to your customer? Is it price or is it quality? What is the competition doing to meet these needs? What can you offer that meets your customers' needs better than the competition is able to do?

Step 2: Learn about your product/service. How will your product/service meet the needs of your customer? Why is your product/service a better solution than the competitors?

Step 3: Put yourself in your customer's position. If you were the customer, why would you choose the product or service you are offering?

Develop your belief base. After you have done steps 1 through 3, question your belief base. How much do you believe? Is it head knowledge only or do you believe in your heart? There is a Bible passage that says, "Out of the abundance of the heart, the mouth speaks." If you believe, more of your potential customers will believe and buy!

Zig Ziglar said,

> "If you can dream it, then you can achieve it. You will get all you want in life if you help enough other people get what they want."

There are a couple of points here many people miss. Dreaming comes first. It is OK to dream. Think about what you will do with all the money you are going to make. Just don't forget to turn your dream into a plan of action. Second, notice the words "enough other people." How many is enough?

My first competitive sales job was for the High School band. Not only did I win the competition, I outsold the rest of the band combined. For years I thought I was a natural born salesperson. The truth was I simply outworked my competition and called on more prospective customers than anyone else did.

Here is a key point.

"You can hone your skills while you are calling on customers. The more you call on, the more likely you are to make a sale. The more sales you make, the better your skills will become."

If you will forget about becoming discouraged because someone turns you down by making calls until your closing ratio improves. As you turn it into a learning experience you will have the fortitude to keep closing ratio improves, your attitude and passion grows and the money in the bank grows. You choose whether to make a "no" from the customer a stepping-stone to success or the beginning of a downward spiral to discouragement and defeat.

Passion can overcome any obstacle. Fill your attitude with passion for your products and services. Overflow your attitude with passion for your customer. It will yield an abundance of income. Abundance means you have more than enough to meet your needs! I can get passionate about that!

To find out if this is the right business for you, call or write to us today.

WL Laney (303) 217-8660 Ext 3 or email WL at WL@diamondroseshears.com

www.ingramcontent.com/pod-product-compliance
Lightning Source LLC
Chambersburg PA
CBHW071811170526
45167CB00003B/1271